5/23/98

To Ellen – on your first communion day.
God loves you and we do too.
Love,
Grandma and Grandpa R.

Just Goldens

Just Goldens

PHOTOGRAPHS BY DALE C. SPARTAS
TEXT BY TOM DAVIS

WILLOW CREEK PRESS

MINOCQUA, WISCONSIN

Peanuts cartoon on Page 8 reprinted by permission of United Feature Syndicate, Inc.

Published by WILLOW CREEK PRESS, P.O. Box 147, Minocqua, WI 54548

For information on other Willow Creek titles, write or call 1-800-850-WILD

Individual custom prints of the photographs in this book are available for purchase directly from the photographer. Write to: Dale C. Spartas, 1120 Nelson Road, Bozeman, MT 59715, or call (406) 585-2244 or FAX (406) 585-0038.

Library of Congress Cataloging-in-Publication Data

Spartas, Dale C.
    Just goldens / photographs by Dale C. Spartas ; text by Tom Davis.
        p.   cm.
    ISBN 1-57223-041-X (alk. paper)
    1. Golden retrievers. 2. Golden retrievers–
Pictorial works.   I. Davis, Tom, 1956- .   II. Title
SF429.G63S63   1996
636.7'52–dc20   96-32598
                                           CIP

Printed in Canada

Contents

Introduction

Several years ago, on a curiously mild February evening, I found myself sitting on the hood of a rental car, watching the sun go down over Chesapeake Bay. It was pretty unremarkable, as sunsets go, but it suited my mood. I'll spare you the details; the bottom line, though, is that the you-know-what had been hitting the fan for a long time, and I was about one more piece of bad news from becoming a prescription-carrying member of Prozac Nation. A magazine had dispatched me to the Eastern Shore of Maryland to gather material for a story, and while I didn't particularly want to be there, the fact of the matter is that I didn't particularly want to be anywhere.

That's when the golden retriever materialized. And I do mean materialized: Suddenly, he was just there, standing on the left side of the car, deliberately wagging his thickly feathered tail and proffering a stick that happened to be the perfect size for throwing. He was a fine-looking animal, rangy but strongly built, with alert, intelligent eyes, a coat the color of a freshly minted penny, and a breezy, self-assured air. Given the locale, and its rich wildfowling tradition, I had no doubt that he was a true working retriever, that he was no stranger to frosty dawns and icy seas, to cramped layout boats and crude goose pits, to bluebills and black ducks, canvasbacks and Canadas.

The offer was one I couldn't refuse, so I swung down from the hood of the car, took the stick, and lobbed it end-over-end into the murmuring surf. A smooth, powerful swimmer, the golden retrieved it promptly. We kept the game up for a few minutes, until, as if he had another appointment to keep, the copper dog shook himself, picked up his stick, and trotted jauntily down the road – like the proverbial kid who takes his bat and ball and goes home.

Watching him saunter off, his flag swishing merrily, I became aware that something had changed. I couldn't quite put my finger on it, and then it hit me: For the first time in months, I felt unconditionally happy. The gloom had burned off, the weight had magically lifted, there was reason to be optimistic again. It was as if I'd shucked a dry old skin. I realized that I was smiling, and that it was thanks to a golden retriever whose name I'd never know, but who buoyed my spirits in a way I'd never forget.

Well, make of it what you will. I, for one, am a firm believer in the therapeutic value of playing fetch-the-stick with a golden retriever. But then, I don't know that any breed is as reliably *simpatico* as the golden. Goldens have an uncanny – and occasionally spooky – ability to tune into your mood and provide whatever cheer, comfort, and/or solace you require. It might be as small a gesture as nudging your hand with a soft, gentle muzzle, or laying a beautiful head in your lap – but it makes all the difference in the world. A woman may need a man like a fish needs a bicycle, but there are times when *everyone* needs a golden retriever.

Of course, it's hard to talk about goldens without bringing up Labradors. Both are retrieving breeds, obviously, and both are hugely popular. In terms of temperament, however, they're oceans apart. It's almost as if they represent the two sides of the human brain, or the Type A/Type B personality dichotomy. (This makes absolute sense when you consider that the various dog breeds are, ultimately, the products of man's relentless urge to tinker.) The Lab is the left side, Type A dog: logical, driven, intensely goal oriented. If Labs were people, they'd be surgeons, accountants, attorneys, and CEOs – successful, yes, but a little, um, predictable.

Goldens, in contrast, are right side, Type B dogs: imaginative, mellow, enemies of routines. They'd be dancers, musicians, poets, artists – quirky, fun-loving, and full of surprises. You'd want a Labrador to handle your money, but you'd want a golden to throw your party. A couple hours into the festivities, it'd be the one wearing the lampshade.

Make no mistake, though: This dog hunts. The same golden that romps in the backyard and gets ice cream cones with the rest of the family on warm summer nights becomes a gundog *par excellence* when the redleg mallards wing down from the north country and the rooster pheasants are in their glossy, brassy prime.

It was my privilege, for a goodly span of years, to gun over a truly marvelous golden retriever named

April. She belonged to my friend Erik "Roscoe" Forsgren, and she was as tenacious and indefatigable a four-footed hunter as I've ever busted brush behind. There wasn't an ounce of quit in her; plus, she had a nose that was nothing short of astonishing. One retrieve in particular, on a wing-tipped South Dakota cockbird that had been given up for lost, has become the stuff of legend in certain bird hunting circles.

For the record, April's nose was equally keen when it came to detecting cookies, sandwiches, and other goodies. The oatmeal raisin cookies from the bakery in Crivitz, Wisconsin, were her favorites.

April's gone now, but she's never far from mind — especially on those frosty autumn nights when the woodcock, like spirits felt but unseen, are navigating south by the stars and the ice melts slowly in our glasses of highland malt. And while the jury's still out on the heiress to her mantle, Ilsa (named for the Ingrid Bergman character in *Casablanca*, but commonly referred to as the She-Devil), the evidence suggests that she's got what it takes. This much is guaranteed: As hard and as often as Erik hunts, she'll enjoy plenty of opportunities to hone her skills. I even hear that Erik's buying a new duckboat, just for Ilsa — or at least that's the spin he puts on it when his wife's in the same room.

But whether you hunt your golden or not, it's important to remember that this heritage, in the final analysis, is responsible for the wonderful qualities — the very ones celebrated in Dale Spartas' photographs — that give the breed its universal appeal. The intelligence, the sensitivity, the warmth, the athleticism so eloquently expressed in Dale's images, were developed and refined by many generations of breeding for *function*, not merely for appearance or, even more craven, simply to supply the demand. As unbelievable as it may sound, there are goldens today that display about as much retrieving instinct as the average Schnauzer.

At the risk of putting words into Dale's mouth, I don't think he spent nearly two decades lugging a battery of heavy cameras around in order to take photographs that would end up being primarily of interest to historians. It behooves everyone, breeders and buyers alike, to insist upon the highest standards, standards that will preserve the golden we love, admire, and trust.

After all, you never know when you'll need a buddy to play fetch-the-stick with.

– Tom Davis,
Baileys Harbor, Wisconsin

Dedication

I dedicate this book to my four wonderful children,
Kaitlin, Elizabeth, Sarah and Christo,
whose innocence, beauty, idealism and love
have added immeasurably to life's quality.

– D.C.S.

Acknowledgements

I'd like to acknowledge the following people for their time, patience, support and beautiful goldens. Bill Baldus & Buck, Bev Bellehuemer & Dusty, Amy Branson & Honey, The Brewster Family, Tom Butler & April, Ken Conger & Libby, Byron Dugree & Reb, Chuck Forest Craig Janssen, Ed Gerrity and Flying Falcon Kennels, Gwen & Lakota, Bob Goodwillie & Rusty, Roper Green & Grizz, Jeff Herbert & Tanker, Joe Kerchinski & Gunner, M.B. Kolarchek, Ken Nielsen & Brody, Donna Pace, Amy & Autumn Peterson & Bow, Jennifer Petrusha & Buster, Ken Raynor, Jack Risselman & Snickers, Dale Sexton, Gary Smith & Addie, Tom and Pat Stonehouse & Casey, Rick Wollum & Ranier, and everyone else who has helped with this project.

PORTRAITS

Aristocrats –
With the Common Touch

The old dog knows; the young dogs want to. Natural inquisitiveness and intelligence are where the journey to wisdom begins, but only the long road of experience can put that soulful, knowing look in a golden's eyes.

H as anyone ever met a golden retriever they didn't like? Or walked past one on the street without stopping to scratch a silky ear, the dog leaning into the pressure of your touch, its eyes half-closed in bliss? If ever a breed was affectionate to a fault, it's the golden. They're people dogs, pure and simple, and if you own one there's never any doubt that you're the center of its universe. Chances are, too, that it will become the center of yours. Golden owners and their dogs didn't invent the mutual admiration society – they perfected it.

G oldens aren't often recommended as watchdogs. They're too darn friendly, more apt to greet a trespasser with a wagging tail and come-hither smile than with bristling hackles and low growls that clearly mean business. Every once in a while, though, you encounter a golden whose stare alone carries a pretty emphatic message: *You're on my turf, pal, and you'd better mind your p's and q's.*

LIVING WITH GOLDENS

*Darlings, Rogues
and Rascals*

N
o book about dogs
would be complete
without some doggerel,
so here goes:

It flies through the air
With the greatest of ease:
The golden retriever
Trained to chase down Frisbees.

F rom zero . . .

. . . to sixty.

T he golden's even temperament and happy-go-lucky personality mask a desire to retrieve that, when the match is struck, burns with white-hot intensity.

The dog books all agree that goldens are, quote, "enthusiastic retrievers from both land and water," It's been said so often, in fact, that it's

become a cliche. But just because a statement is cliche
doesn't mean it isn't correct.

Goldens aren't particular about *what* they retrieve. A training dummy is fine – but so is a ball, a stick, a ripe, dead carp, or Dad's favorite pair of slippers. And if there's a chance to mix in a quick game of keep-away, so much the better.

Professional trainers – which is to say, people in a position to know – will tell you that goldens tend to be "thinkers" as opposed to "doers." In other words, they like to mull things over and consider their options before choosing an appropriate course of action. This independence of mind occasionally puts them at loggerheads with their human partners. (One of the most legendary "incidents" in field trial history occurred when a champion golden and its handler had a difference of opinion regarding the proper sequence in which to accomplish a test that required multiple retrieves.) It also explains why you don't really *command* a golden. First, you define your terms; then, you coax, cajole and cross your fingers. Any way you cut it, though, possession is still nine-tenths of the law.

O f course, some retrieves are more problematic than others. The job usually gets done – but the integrity of the retrieved object can't always be guaranteed.

Y ou can't play as hard as golden retrievers do without indulging in regular siestas. They don't need much provocation, either. A little exercise, a warm patch of sunshine, and it's snooze city, baby. Generations of goldens have refined napping into an art form.

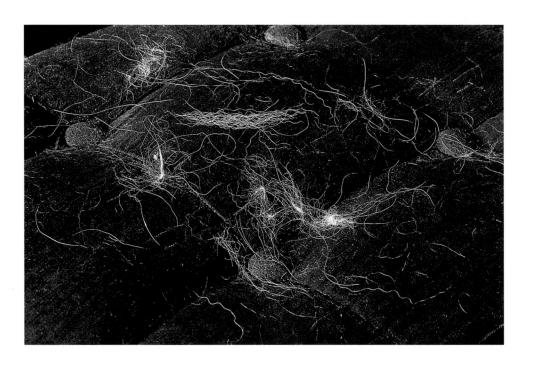

Beauty, as they say, has its price. The golden's luxurious coat requires serious upkeep: shampooing, combing, brushing, de-burring. Still, most goldens – and their owners – seem to enjoy these rituals of vanity. And if fussy friends comment about the dog hair that finds its way onto (and into) everything in sight, maybe it's time to get new friends.

W henever possible, goldens prefer being with people – specifically, with *their* people. They chafe at being confined or, even worse, left behind, and on the occasions when they're instructed to stay put, you can almost see the smoke coming out of their ears. ("Leave *me* in the car, after all we've been through together? Why, you ungrateful !@#$%! I'll fix *your* wagon.") No one ever said that goldens couldn't be willful – or, for that matter, downright hard-headed. Funny thing is, it makes you love them all the more.

G oldens can be frustrating, irritating, even exasperating. But all it takes is a certain look – a cock of the ear, a furrow in the brow – to smooth things over, put the smile back on your face, and fill your heart with joy. No one stays mad at a golden retriever for very long.

In every life, a little rain must fall. A golden retriever is an umbrella with soul, a friend you can count on no matter how tough the going gets. Lost your job? The love of your life ran off with your neighbor? Your golden's there for you, pilgrim.

Goldens are poor choices for people uncomfortable with public displays of affection. It wouldn't be far wrong to call them brazen. Big, wet, sloppy kisses are their stock-in-trade, and while you grimace when you receive one, it's really just to conceal your delight.

S ome dogs are content with an occasional pat on the head and a briefly expressed term of endearment. Not goldens – they demand the maximum dosage. They bask in attention, wallow in it, soak it up like a sponge. Fair's fair, after all: You can't expect them to dish out those heaping portions of the sweet stuff unless they're enjoying a steady diet of it themselves.

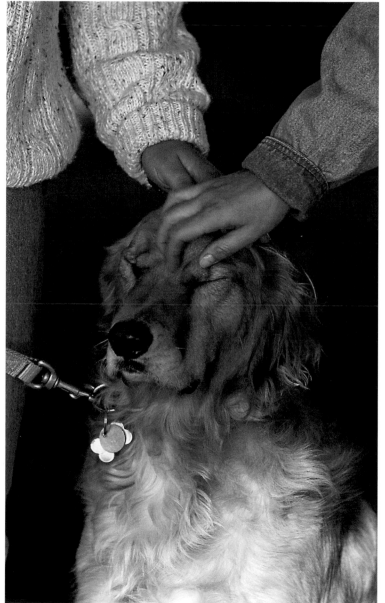

The dress code for walking goldens can be summed up in one word: casual. As good as they make you look (and feel), you could throw on the rattiest clothes in your dresser and anyone who saw you would swear you'd stepped right out of a Ralph Lauren ad. This fact has not been lost on Madison Avenue.

L ike celestial bodies, golden retrievers exert a kind of gravitational attraction. It's a virtual law of nature that a solitary golden will soon have company, pulling passersby into its orbit.

G oldens don't have to be told that they're just a
little better than other dogs; they know. They're
not above gently lording their superiority over
the less fortunate members of canine society, either.

For decades, it was believed that the golden Retriever was descended from mysterious "Russian circus dogs" that Lord Tweedmouth,

the acknowledged father of the breed, purchased circa 1860. Only in 1952, when Tweedmouth's detailed records were discovered, was this account

revealed to be a complete hoax, perpetrated by unknown pranksters who, to quote the late Richard Wolters, "must have giggled all the way to their graves." Still, there's no denying that goldens are born show-offs. They're shameless hams, and they relish an audience. It almost

makes you wonder if one of those Russian circus dogs didn't manage to scale the fence at Lord Tweedmouth's kennel.

As far as the average golden retriever is concerned, its status as a member of the "sporting" category is inclusive of *all* outdoor pursuits, not just hunting. It must be admitted, however, that its role as a fishing

dog is largely supervisory. And part of being a good supervisor is knowing when to stick your nose in, and when to butt out, close the office door, and tell the secretary to hold your calls.

SPORTING COMPANIONS

*The Ancient
Partnership
Endures*

Getting there is half the fun – especially when your destination is a hidden, jewel-like pond that only you, and your golden, know about. It's one of the little secrets you share, part of the private territory of your sporting partnership. The two of you could find your way there in the dark, and often do, crunching through the snow in the bitter, pre-dawn chill, your breath like a hovering ghost. Nothing need be said; you're occupying old, familiar roles, and you're connected by the bright filament of a primal calling.

The easy-going attitude displayed around the house vanishes once the hunt is on. This is serious business, fraught with such critical decisions as the proper placement of the decoys. And, because you're partners in this, you can almost hear your golden putting in his two cents' worth: "A little more to the right . . . a little more . . . too far . . . perfect." It's almost as if an interior decorating gene snuck in there somewhere.

Waterfowl hunting is essentially a waiting game. You try to select an appealing spot, arrange the decoys temptingly, and make beautiful music with your calls, but whether the birds come in or not is

ultimately up to them. At least, when you're waiting with a golden retriever, you're in enjoyable company. The conversation tends to be a little one-sided, though.

E
verything that the golden is begins with this: the irresistible desire to retrieve, to find downed game and *bring it back*. It's a miracle, really, an irrevocably encoded behavior that, taken out of context, seems like an amusing parlor trick. But to a waterfowl hunter, it's the *sine qua non*, the olive in the martini, the distilled and potent essence of the sport.

When gunner and golden have each done their part, an honest pride wells up – a pride that is palpable and satisfying as a drake mallard in the hand.

T
he golden is such a devilishly handsome fellow that it's easy to forget that form follows function. That thick, luxurious, altogether gorgeous coat, for example, is meant to shed water, insulate against the cold, and blend in with the pale reeds and rushes of a winter marsh. Think of it as blonde camouflage.

Goldens are true all-purpose gundogs. Their tastes are catholic; if it has feathers, they'll hunt it and pick it up. Those who gun over goldens are rarely in a hurry for the bird to be delivered to hand. They'd just as soon let their dog strike a pose and hold it for a while, so they can savor the moment and admire the auxtaposition of beauty.

At some point in the dim and distant past, man quit kidding himself and concluded that, as predators go, he left a lot to be desired. He was slow; he was clumsy; his senses were dull. To his credit, though, he had brains enough to recruit the dog as his ally. It was one of the shrewdest moves *homo sapiens* ever made. The dog became his eyes, ears and, particularly, his nose; a tougher, faster, more courageous extension of himself. This alliance was thousands of years old by the time the golden entered the picture – but there are those who would argue that it's never been closer to perfection. They're the people who hunt with golden retrievers.

It is not the kill that the hunter lives for, but for those luminous moments that burn their images into his memory, the vastness of time and space, past and present condensed to this: a golden retriever, a brilliant, cackling

rooster, and a certain quality of light. Comes the darkness, when you drift away
to sleep, this is the vessel you sail into the sea of dreams.

Although they dominated the sport during its formative era, goldens are no longer a major factor in retriever field trials. To the legions of sportsmen whose hard-hunting goldens are, to their way of thinking, uncrowned champions, this has as much practical relevance as the fact that the sun will someday burn out.

O h, the boundless energy of youth! The muscles like coiled springs of tempered steel, the enthusiasm as hot and bright as the blue flame from a welder's torch. Young dogs can ride this wave of adrenaline from dawn 'til dusk, never tiring (hell, never drawing a deep breath!), letting nothing stand in their purposeful way. Whatever they lack in technique, they make up for in sheer drive, in ferocious determination. And when you're feeling bone-weary yourself, they pull you along in the slipstream.

Muddy Waters used to sing (as only Muddy could) about how young horses are fast, but old horses know what's going on. It's the same with old goldens: There's no wasted motion, no frivolity, just a job to be done, and a hard-edged, professional way of doing it. Wisdom is the compensation for the erosion of the body. Of course, a poignant aura surrounds any hunt with a grizzled, gray-muzzled veteran, a dog with whom you share a history, a dog that has taught you things — about birds, about living, about yourself — that you never understood before. But that's between the two of you, as private and personal as the contents of a diary.

PUPPIES!

Simply Irresistible

Whoever coined the term "warm fuzzies" to describe a feeling of complete contentment must have had golden retriever puppies in mind. They're simply irresistible, and they have a smell — musky, damp, sweet-sour — like nothing else on earth.

There is no such thing as window-shopping for a golden retriever puppy. You may have the best intentions of "just looking" when you go to check out a litter, but the fact of the matter is that as soon as you lay eyes on those frolicking, floppy-eared bundles of yellow fur, your goose is cooked. One of the puppies will meet your gaze with a smile that reaches all the way to your heart, a smile that says "I'm the one. Take *me* home." And you will. You irrevocably, joyfully, and certainly will.

Physics teachers devote hours of class time to explaining the concepts of potential energy and kinetic energy, as well as the relationship between the two. A field trip to visit a litter of goldens would achieve the same result – and be a heck of a lot more fun. Plus, you'd have to memorize just two equations: Potential energy = Golden puppies in a pen; Kinetic energy = Golden puppies on the loose. There would also be a natural tie-in to the law stating that bodies in motion tend to stay in motion.

The capacity of puppies to engage in mock combat seems limitless. Suddenly, one gets that mischievous gleam in its eye and pounces on the nearest available littermate, its jaws clamping down on whatever tender body part gets in the way. These contests are surprisingly fierce: The fur flies, the teeth flash like drawn knives, and big, menacing growls emerge from those little, adorable throats. They wrestle, roll one over the other, disengage, shake, and come back for more. A clear-cut victor can rarely be identified, and if pride is wounded, there's always a rematch to look forward to.

For puppies, as for children, one of the most important lessons to learn is where the lines are – and which ones shouldn't be crossed. Another important lesson – respect for one's elders – comes with the territory.

Puppies and mud go together like Astaire and Rogers, bourbon and branch, leather and lace. This goes a long way toward explaining why puppies and carpets are usually a bad mix.

S uch declarations are always subject to debate, but a strong case can be made that the golden retriever has brought more happiness to more children than any other breed.

G oldens are the original chow-hounds. If you're packing anything edible, you can run – but you can't hide. They'll sniff you out, surround you, and make you surrender the goods. Your picture might as well be on display at the post office.

At last, there comes a day when the pup's mettle must be tested. You can't wait any longer; you have to find out if the raw material, the right stuff, is there. You're on pins and needles as you lob the training dummy, hoping, wondering . . . And the pup – awkward, uncoordinated, but intensely focused – gallops out, grabs the dummy as best it can, and proudly brings it back. Once again, the legacy of blood, of breeding, has been proven. Was there really any doubt?

Needless to say, you don't truly *train* a puppy to retrieve. It comes naturally; the desire is hard-wired into their genetic circuitry. Your role is to refine and perfect this desire, using such tools as repetition, association, and praise. It helps to have an eager pupil, too, and a well-bred golden puppy will hang on your every word.

Nothing is safe from a puppy's teeth. They're stiletto sharp – like tiny ivory daggers – and every opportunity to employ them is seized. Shoelaces, pants cuffs, and other floppy, dangly, eye-level items make tempting targets, but everything is ultimately fair game. Wherever a puppy looks, it sees a sign that reads, *Chew Here.*

What is a golden retriever puppy?
The stuff that dreams are made of
– the sweetest dreams of all.